WRITERS

ON ...

NATURE

AMELIA CARRUTHERS

CONTENTS

INTRODUCTION

Nature writing is a genre born out of love, reverence and wonder at the natural world. It is an attempt, like all creative endeavours, to reconcile 'truth' with personal interpretation, and through writing – the very embodiment of human separation from the animal kingdom – to reawaken our connections with nature. Herein lie the contradictions, challenges, yet also rewards of this highly captivating genre.

Although the environment has been a constant source of fascination for poets, playwrights and prosaicists alike, 'nature writing' proper only fully emerged in the early nineteenth century. As Michael P. Branch, one of America's leading scholars on the subject has emphasised, the term is 'usually reserved for a brand of nature representation that is deemed literary, written in the speculative personal voice, and presented in the form of the non-fiction essay. Such nature writing is frequently pastoral or romantic in its philosophical assumptions, tends to be modern or even ecological in its sensibility, and is often in service to an explicit or implicit preservationist agenda.'

Nature writing is so much more than 'creative non-fiction' though – it is an expression of one's individual relationship with the landscape, resulting from days, weeks, months or years of close observation of the natural world. It is a baton which has been passed on for thousands of years. To early civilisations, nature was absolutely vital for their survival – hunting wild animals and foraging plants was part of everyday life. Nature was a force little understood, yet much respected, linked as much with the heavens as it was with the earth. Early monuments such as Germany's Goseck circle and England's Stonehenge are a testament to ancient civilisation's attempts to understand the natural world, but it was not until the proliferation of scholarly endeavour in ancient Chinese and Greek civilisations that 'natural histories' and 'natural philosophies' really started to emerge.

Natural Philosophy has more in common with today's sciences; physics, biology and chemistry, than strictly literary nature writing. But it is an important forebear of the tradition of respect and almost mystical veneration that we see in many later works. For the Greeks, and the Romans too, understanding nature was one of the highest modes of study, and one that would unlock knowledge of the earth, the deities that created it and, therefore, humans too. The concepts of *natural law* and *natural justice,* as exemplified by Aristotle, the Stoics and Cicero shaped subsequent European law and culture – and thus laid the foundations for our current relationship with nature. Scholars such as Plutarch and Pliny exemplified the practice of nature writing as we know it, Pliny by composing the first known encyclopaedia – *Naturalis Historia,* and Plutarch who made the case for linking naturalism, vegetarianism and environmentalism; a tenet held dear by many subsequent nature writers. In the great ancient Chinese cultures, nature held a more directly spiritual position. Living in harmony with nature, following the *Tao* (the driving force behind everything that exists) was at the centre of Taoist wisdom and many ensuing theories of our place in the universe.

Religious texts have long taken nature as a starting point for comprehending the self in the wider world. Nature is the most visible and tangible evidence of any deities' works, and thus a window into divine creation. Whilst the great monotheistic religions preach of man's privileged position at the top of the natural hierarchy, they also stress imperative responsibilities as custodian and carer of the environment. This complex relationship is furthered in many Eastern belief systems as well as Native American shamanism, which teach of the inextricable links between man and the landscape – crucially *as part of,* as opposed to *separate from* nature. Such concerns have rippled across the ages, and have informed much of the transcendentalist writings, epitomised by American authors such as Henry David Thoreau, Ralph Waldo Emerson and John Muir. Transcendentalism is best understood as both a religious and a philosophical movement, which developed in the late 1820s as a protest against unquestioning scientific intellectualism. Thoreau especially believed that society and its institutions (particularly organised religion and political parties) ultimately corrupt the purity of the individual. A person is 'at their best' when they are truly self-reliant and independent; at one with their natural surroundings and means of support.

Whilst laudable to many, such principled aims and beliefs have meant that nature writing and nature writers have not always been universally popular (not least among themselves!). As a group, they have been accused of bourgeois escapism, anthropomorphism, whimsical fantasy, as nationalists, jingoists and fascists, even for *falsely* idealising the natural world. Across the Atlantic, John Clare, the 'Northamptonshire Peasant Poet' famously lambasted Keats for his romantic (and importantly *metropolitan*) sentimentality. Clare argued that Keats had destroyed the integrity of our relationship with the countryside, representing 'nature as she... appeared in his fancy's and not as he would have described her if he had *witnessed* the things he describes.' (Note here a distinct link with the Christian concept of *witness* – sharing one's *heartfelt* faith.) The American author John Burroughs similarity attacked his fellow naturalists, Ernest Thompson Seton and William J. Long, for what he saw as 'fantastical representations of wildlife.' This became the *Nature Fakers Controversy* of 1903, which involved leading environmental and political figures of the day, including President Theodore Roosevelt, who was a close friend of Burroughs.

Although many did, and still do disagree with the indictments of Clare and Burroughs – they raise a fundamental aspect of nature writing; that of a personal connection with the subject matter. The stress on 'subject' as opposed to 'object' is a key motivation for many naturalists. It signals an innate respect for the landscape and its inhabitants – as active subject, rather than passive object. This latter attitude, seeking to scientifically describe the natural world is better termed 'natural history writing'; a significant, though entirely different genre to literary naturalism. Nature writing differs in that it locates nature's wonders at the *centre* of the author's vision, appreciated for its own intrinsic nature, rather than as a set of data to be comprehended.

Despite the recurrent aspect of *subjectivity*, 'commonality' is an exceptionally hard term to apply to nature writing. The only other constant (although this could be debated) is an 'anti-pastoral' attitude. Contrary to popular depictions, naturalists tend to eschew idyllic pastoral scenes. Like Clare, many see such depictions as falsely idealised, created predominantly for urban audiences. Instead, most nature writing repudiates the affectedly quaint character of such 'back-to-nature' attitudes and celebrates our own innate experience – again, *as part of* the landscape. Nature writing is importantly localised and wild. It is to be found in the small and particular, and whilst universalised and philosophical observations can be made, the direction of travel is *from the particular to the general*. Here, the inductive reasoning of the British empiricists, led by Sir Francis Bacon played a decisive role.

Although it was in America that nature writing as a literary genre really took off, the Reverend Gilbert White, a resident of Selborne, England, penned one of the first 'nature novels.' This was the *Natural History and Antiquities of Selborne* (1789), compiled from a mixture of his own observations, letters to other naturalists and celebration of the particularity of his sleepy Hampshire town. In the late eighteenth century, this approach was revolutionarily modern – an epistolary text which showed the same respect to insects, birds and hedgerows as it did to human residents and holy buildings. White's lifelong friend John Mulso wrote to him in 1776, correctly predicting that 'Your work, upon the whole, will immortalize your Place of Abode as well as Yourself.' John Clare and Eliza Brightwen can perhaps be identified as his successors; Clare the 'peasant poet' who championed his birthplace of Helpston – its local countryside, common folk and animal inhabitants; and Brightwen, a self taught, reclusive naturalist who conducted much of her research at her home, 'The Grove.'

Contemporary nature writing traces its roots to such works of natural history, including other, more scientific texts popular in the eighteenth and nineteenth centuries; those of William Bartram, John James Audubon, Charles Darwin,

Richard Jefferies and other explorers, collectors and naturalists. Henry David Thoreau is often considered the father of American nature writing, conceived by many as the apogee of the genre. Like the writings of William Wordsworth and the Romantic tradition, Thoreau's nature writing teaches the reader as much about the author as its does the specificity of *Walden Pond* or the woods of Maine. This powerful tradition has continued throughout the American, British and European variants of the genre, from Mary Hunter Austin's lyrical depictions of the High Sierra and the Mojave Desert of southern California, to Walt Whitman's humanistic epic the *Leaves of Grass,* and Edward Thomas's poetry – placing plants on a par with pharaohs.

As is evident from this brief introduction to the genre of *nature writing*, it is an incredibly diverse tradition with long historical roots, cherished as much today as it was at its eighteenth century beginnings. The natural world has held writers in its sway for centuries, and remains a source of sustenance and support; spiritually, physically and intellectually. As the following excerpts and quotations will demonstrate, it is a genre which facilitates self-awareness as much as outward knowledge, taking equal care over the large and the small. Happy wandering.

UNDERSTANDING NATURE

NO MAN EVER STEPS IN THE SAME RIVER TWICE.

– Heraclitus (c. 535–c. 475 BCE), a pre-Socratic Greek Philosopher. From the lonely life he led, and still more from the riddling and paradoxical nature of his philosophy, Heraclitus was dubbed 'The Obscure' and the 'Weeping Philosopher.' He was renowned for his insistence on ever-present change in the universe – a theme which is elaborated in much nature writing today.

He is richest who is content with the least, for content is the wealth of nature.

– Socrates (470/469–399 BCE); one of the founders of Western Philosophy. Such ideas went on to influence the practice of 'Simple Living' (distinct from the more spiritual *asceticism*). The concept has since inspired renowned naturalists such as Ralph Waldo Emerson, Aldo Leopold, and Henry David Thoreau – most famously described in Thoreau's book *Walden* (1854).

IN ALL THINGS OF NATURE THERE IS SOMETHING OF THE MARVELLOUS.

– Aristotle (384–322 BCE), *Parts of Animals*, Book I, 645.a16.

What nature is . . . has been stated. That nature exists, it would be absurd to try to prove; for it is obvious that there are many things of this kind, and to prove what is obvious by what is not is the mark of a man who is unable to distinguish what is self-evident from what is not.

Physics II, 193a3.

Nature does nothing uselessly.

Politics, Book I, 1253.a8.

– Aristotle (384–322 BCE), who studied under Plato (who had studied under Socrates in turn), and later became tutor to Alexander the Great. His views, especially on the natural world profoundly shaped medieval and renaissance scholarship, and show just how fascinating 'nature' was to early civilisations.

It is impossible for someone to dispel his fears about the most important matters if he doesn't know the nature of the universe but still gives some credence to myths. So without the study of nature there is no enjoyment of pure pleasure.

– Epicurus (341–270 BCE), who founded the Greek school of philosophy known as *Epicureanism*. For Epicurus, the purpose of philosophy was to attain a happy, peaceful and painless life – which could be achieved by understanding the natural world, living modestly and limiting one's desires. Epicurus' ideas have remained influential into the present day, and deeply influenced the American naturalist, Ralph Waldo Emerson in his assertion that 'a great man is always willing to be little.'

First of all, Nature has endowed every species of living

creature with the instinct of self-preservation, of avoiding what

seems likely to cause injury to life or limb, and of procuring

and providing everything needful for life — food, shelter,

and the like.... There is, however, no such thing as private

ownership established by nature.

– Cicero (106–43 BCE), *De Officiis (44 BCE)*. Cicero's writings on natural law and innate
rights helped shape the great structures of Roman law, which in turn influenced Western
political liberties as we know them. As 'nature' did not protect private property of the
individual, this became one of government's primary purposes. Henry David Thoreau
later argued specifically against private property in nature, in his essay *Walking* (1862).

And yet it is hard to believe that anything

in nature could stand revealed as solid matter.

The lightning of heaven goes through the walls of houses,

like shouts and speech; iron glows white in fire;

red-hot rocks are shattered by savage steam;

hard gold is softened and melted down by heat;

chilly brass, defeated by heat, turns liquid;

heat seeps through silver, so does piercing cold;

by custom raising the cup, we feel them both

as water is poured in, drop by drop, above.

– Lucretius (99–55 BCE) was a Roman poet and philosopher, fascinated by the natural world. His only known work is the epic philosophical poem, *De Rerum Natura* ('On the Nature of Things'), quoted above.

My subject is a barren one—the world of nature, or in other words, 'life'. [...]
The path is not a beaten highway of authorship, nor one in which the mind is
eager to range: there is not one person to be found among us who has made
the same venture, nor yet one among the Greeks who has tackled single-handed
all departments of the subject. A large part of us seek agreeable fields of study,
while topics of immeasurable abstruseness treated by others are drowned in the
shadowy darkness of the theme. [...] It is a difficult task to give novelty to what is
old, authority to what is new, brilliance to the common-place, light to the obscure,
attraction to the stale, credibility to the doubtful, but nature to all things and
all her properties to nature. Accordingly, even if we have not succeeded, it is
honourable and glorious in the fullest measure to have resolved on the attempt.

– Pliny the Elder (23–79 CE) was quite possibly one of the first 'naturalists' as we now
understand the term. He spent most of his spare time studying, writing or investigating
natural and geographic phenomena, and wrote the encyclopaedic *Naturalis Historia*
('Natural History'), which has became a model for all other encyclopaedias since.

It is certainly not lions and wolves that we eat out of self-defence; on the contrary, we ignore these and slaughter harmless, tame creatures without stings or teeth to harm us, creatures that, I swear, Nature appears to have produced for the sake of their beauty and grace. But nothing abashed us, not the flower-like tinting of the flesh, not the persuasiveness of the harmonious voice, not the cleanliness of their habits or the unusual intelligence that may be found in the poor wretches. No, for the sake of a little flesh we deprive them of sun, of light, of the duration of life to which they are entitled by birth and being.

– Plutarch (46–120 CE) was Greek (and later Roman) historian, biographer and essayist. This passage aptly demonstrates the time-honoured links between naturalism, environmentalism and vegetarianism. A key part of nature writing is an inherent respect and curiosity for the environment; its landscape, vegetation and the living creatures that call it home.

RELIGION ON NATURE

Nature does not hurry,
yet everything is accomplished.

– Lao-Tzu (usually dated to around the 6th century BCE), was a philosopher and a poet of ancient China, best known as the reputed author of the *Tao Te Ching* and the founder of philosophical Taoism. Lao-Tzu is also revered as a deity in religious Taoism and many traditional Chinese religions, which emphasise living in harmony with the *Tao* (meaning 'path' or 'principle' – something that is both the source and driving force behind everything that exists).

Consider the lilies, how they grow: they neither toil nor spin, yet I tell you, even Solomon in all his glory was not arrayed like one of these.

– *The Bible*, Luke 12:27. Historically, naturalism has had a strong spiritual aspect. As evidenced in Greek and Roman scholarship – understanding nature was seen as part way to understanding oneself. These early theological texts provide a fascinating insight into the complex relationship between man as custodian, yet also as child of the environment.

THE LORD GOD TOOK THE MAN AND PUT HIM IN THE GARDEN OF EDEN TO TILL AND KEEP IT.

– The Bible; Genesis 2:15.

O Lord, how manifold are thy works!

In wisdom has thou made them all;

The earth is full of thy creatures.

Yonder is the sea, great and wide,

Which teems with things innumerable,

Living things both small and great.

> – *The Bible*, Psalm 104. Given the belief that God created the universe, and the world
> within it – appreciation of nature enabled Christians to realize the miracles of their
> creator. This viewpoint has been expressed by many naturalists since.

Be praised, my Lord, through all your creatures, especially through my lord Brother Sun, who brings the day; and you give light through him. And he is beautiful and radiant in all his splendour! Of you, Most High, he bears the likeness.

Be praised, my Lord, through Sister Moon and the stars; in the heavens you have made them, precious and beautiful.

Be praised, my Lord, through Brothers Wind and Air, and clouds and storms, and all the weather, through which you give your creatures sustenance.

Be praised, My Lord, through Sister Water; she is very useful, and humble, and precious, and pure.

Be praised, my Lord, through Brother Fire, through whom you brighten the night. He is beautiful and cheerful, and powerful and strong.

Be praised, my Lord, through our sister Mother Earth, who feeds us and rules us, and produces various fruits with coloured flowers and herbs.

– Francis of Assisi (1181/82–1226), *Canticle of the Sun* (1224). Frances of Assisi was an Italian Catholic friar and preacher, known as the patron saint of animals and the environment. A legend illustrating the Saint's humility towards nature contends that while Francis was travelling with some companions, they happened upon a place in the road where birds filled the trees. Francis told his companions to 'wait for me while I go to preach to my sisters the birds.' The birds surrounded him, intrigued by the power of his voice, and not one of them flew away.

Lo! We offered the trust
Unto the heavens and the
Earth and the hills,
But they shrank from bearing it
And were afraid of it
And man assumed it
Lo! He is a tyrant and a fool

– *The Quran*, 33: 72. In a similar manner to Christianity and Judaism, Islam
places humans at the top of the natural hierarchy. Just like the other principal
religious texts, The Quran also contends that humans have a mandate to protect the
natural environment.

Seest thou not that it is Allah Whose praises all beings in the heavens and on earth do celebrate, and the birds (of the air) with wings outspread? Each one knows its own mode of prayer and praise. And Allah knows well all that they do.

– The Quran, 24:41.

Ether, air, fire, water, earth, planets, all creatures, directions, trees and plants, rivers and seas, they are all organs of God's body; remembering this, a devotee respects all species.

– Srimad Bhagavata Mahapurana; 2.2.41. This Hindu teaching epitomises the religion's approach to the natural world – one of intense respect and enjoyment. The many Hindu deities reflect the interconnectedness of the environment itself, reminding all followers that they are part of a wider whole.

Time is endless in thy hands, my lord.
There is none to count thy minutes.

Days and nights pass and ages bloom and fade like flowers.
Thou knowest how to wait.

Thy centuries follow each other perfecting a small wild flower.

We have no time to lose,
and having no time we must scramble for a chance.
We are too poor to be late.

– Rabindranath Tagore (1861–1941), 'Endless Time'. Tagore is considered one of the greatest writers in modern Indian literature – a Bengali poet, novelist and teacher who won the Nobel Prize for Literature in 1913. Like the flower, we are inherently finite, and it will take time-in-perpetuity to perfect this small and wild creation.

A good man is the friend of all living things.

– Mahatma Gandhi (1869–1948); the pre-eminent leader of Indian nationalism in British ruled India, who inspired movements for civil rights and freedom across the world. Ghandi's vision was for a free India based on religious pluralism, and his non-violent civil disobedience was largely inspired by the Hindu teachings of equality and respect for the natural world.

We should understand well that all things are the works of the Great Spirit. We should know that He is within all things: the trees, the grasses, the rivers, the mountains, and all the four-legged animals, and the winged peoples.

– Black Elk (1863–1950). Black Elk was a famous medicine man, warrior and holy man of the Sioux people, who taught of the inextricable links between humans and the environment. Native American wisdom holds that we must act as 'Earth Keepers' – an important cultural mandate that has inspired and influenced many environmentalists and naturalists.

THE SEASONS

How many things by season season'd are, To their
right praise and true perfection!

– William Shakespeare (1564–1616), Portia speaking in *The Merchant of Venice,* Act V,
scene i (1605).

Spring

Though a country be sundered, hills and rivers endure;
And spring comes green again to trees and grasses
Where petals have been shed like tears
And lonely birds have sung their grief.
...After the war-fires of three months,
One message from home is worth a ton of gold.
...I stroke my white hair. It has grown too thin
To hold the hairpins any more.

– Tu Fu (712–770 CE), a prominent Chinese poet of the Tang Dynasty. 'A Spring View'
(c. 750, translated by Witter Bynner in 1920).

Sweet April showers
Do spring May flowers.

– Thomas Tusser (1524–1580), an English poet and farmer, best known for his
instructional poem *A Hundred Good Points of Husbandry* (1557).

Spring, the sweet spring, is the year's pleasant king,
Then blooms each thing, then maids dance in a ring,
Cold doth not sting, the pretty birds do sing:
    Cuckoo, jug-jug, pu-we, to-witta-woo!

The palm and may make country houses gay,
Lambs frisk and play, the shepherds pipe all day,
And we hear aye birds tune this merry lay:
    Cuckoo, jug-jug, pu-we, to-witta-woo!

The fields breathe sweet, the daisies kiss our feet,
Young lovers meet, old wives a-sunning sit,
In every street these tunes our ears do greet:
    Cuckoo, jug-jug, pu-we, to witta-woo!

– Thomas Nashe (1567–1601), considered the greatest of the Elizabethan pamphleteers.
He was also a playwright, poet and satirist. 'Summer's Last Will and Testament' (1600).

Spring drew on... and a greenness grew over those brown beds, which, freshening daily, suggested the thought that Hope traversed them at night, and left each morning brighter traces of her steps. Flowers peeped out amongst the leaves; snow-drops, crocuses, purple auriculas, and golden-eyed pansies.

– Charlotte Brontë (1816–1855), an English novelist and poet, and the eldest of the three Brontë sisters. She published her best known novel, *Jane Eyre* (where this quotation is found) under the pen name 'Currer Bell' in 1847.

Gone were but the Winter,
  Come were but the Spring,
I would go to a covert
  Where the birds sing.

Where in the whitethorn
  Singeth a thrush,
And a robin sings
  In the holly-bush.

Full of fresh scents
  Are the budding boughs
Arching high over
  A cool green house:

Full of sweet scents,
  And whispering air
Which sayeth softly:
  'We spread no snare;

'Here dwell in safety,
  Here dwell alone,
With a clear stream
  And a mossy stone...'

– Christina Rosetti (1830–1894), 'Spring Quiet' from *Verses* (1847).

[...] Wild-flowers and vines and weeds come up through the stones, and partly cover them—
Beyond these I pass,
Far, far in the forest, before I think where I go,
Solitary, smelling the earthy smell, stopping now and then in the silence,
Alone I had thought—yet soon a silent troop gathers around me,
Some walk by my side, and some behind, and some embrace my arms or neck,
They, the spirits of friends, dead or alive—thicker they come, a great crowd, and I in the middle,
Collecting, dispensing, singing in spring, there I wander with them,
Plucking something for tokens—tossing toward whoever is near me;
Here! lilac, with a branch of pine,
Here out of my pocket, some moss which I pull'd off a live-oak in Florida, as it hung trailing down,

Here, some pinks and laurel leaves, and a handful of sage,
And here what I now draw from the water, wading in the pond-side,
(O here I last saw him that tenderly loves me—and returns again, never to separate from me,
And this, O this shall henceforth be the token of comrades—this Calamus-root shall,
Interchange it, youths, with each other! Let none render it back!)
And twigs of maple, and a bunch of wild orange, and chestnut,
And stems of currants, and plum-blows, and the aromatic cedar:
These, I, compass'd around by a thick cloud of spirits,
Wandering, point to, or touch as I pass, or throw them loosely from me,
Indicating to each one what he shall have—giving something to each;
But what I drew from the water by the pond-side, that I reserve,
I will give of it—but only to them that love, as I myself am capable of loving.

– Walt Whitman (1819–1892), 'These I, Singing in Spring' from *Leaves of Grass* (1855).

It was one of those March days when the sun shines hot and the wind blows cold: when it is summer in the light, and winter in the shade.

– Charles Dickens (1812–1870), generally regarded as the greatest Victorian novelist. Pip and Herbert departing by boat, in 'Chapter LIV' *Great Expectations* (1861).

'Is the spring coming?' he said. 'What is it like?'...

'It is the sun shining on the rain and the rain falling on

the sunshine...'

– Frances Hodgson Burnett (1829–1924), *The Secret Garden*, initially published in serial
format starting in the autumn of 1910. It tells the story of a troubled ten-year-old girl
who, on the death of her parents, is sent to live in Yorkshire with her uncle, Archibald
Craven, at Misselthwaite Manor.

Oh, that glorious Wisconsin Wilderness! Everything new and pure in the very prime of the spring when Nature's pulses were beating highest and mysteriously keeping time with our own! Young hearts, young leaves, flowers, animals, the winds and the streams and the sparkling lake all wildly gladly rejoicing together!

– John Muir (1838–1914), *The Story of My Boyhood and Youth* (published 1913). Muir, one of the great American naturalists and conservationists, here recalls his arrival in Wisconsin in 1849, from Dunbar, Scotland. He was eleven years old when his family settled at Fountain Lake Farm, next to a large glacial lake in Marquette County, Michigan.

*It was such a spring day as breathes
into a man an ineffable yearning,
a painful sweetness, a longing that
makes him stand motionless, looking
at the leaves or grass, and fling out his
arms to embrace he knows not what.*

– John Galsworthy (1867–1933), 'The Man of Property', the first book of *The Forsyte Saga* (1922) – a text which chronicles the life and loves of a large upper-middle class English family.

Star and coronal and bell
   April underfoot renews,
And the hope of man as well
   Flowers among the morning dews.

Now the old come out to look,
   Winter past and winter's pains,
How the sky in pool and brook
   Glitters on the grassy plains.

Easily the gentle air
   Wafts the turning season on;
Things to comfort them are there,
   Though 'tis true the best are gone...

– A. E. Housman (1859–1936), 'Spring Morning' from *Last Poems* (1922).

Summer

One swallow does not make a summer, neither does one fine day; similarly one day or brief time of happiness does not make a person entirely happy.

– Aristotle (384–322 BCE), _The Nicomachean Ethics,_ based on notes from his lectures at the Lyceum, which were either edited by or dedicated to Aristotle's son, Nicomachus. It focuses on the Socratic question of how men should _best live._

Gently I stir a white feather fan,
With open shirt sitting in a green wood.
I take off my cap and hang it on a jutting stone;
A wind from the pine-trees trickles on my bare head.

    – Li Po (701–762), who along with his friend Tu Fu, was considered one of the most prominent figures in the flourishing of poetry in the mid-Tang Dynasty, often referred to as the 'Golden Age of China.' 'In the Mountains on a Summer Day' (c. 750, translated by Arthur Waley, 1919).

Middle English:

Svmer is icumen in
Lhude sing cuccu!
Groweþ sed and bloweþ med
and springþ þe wde nu.
Sing cuccu!

Awe bleteþ after lomb,
lhouþ after calue cu,
Bulluc sterteþ, bucke uerteþ.
Murie sing cuccu!
Cuccu, cuccu,
Wel singes þu cuccu.
ne swik þu nauer nu!
Sing cuccu nu, Sing cuccu!

Modern English:

Summer has come in
Loudly sing, cuckoo!
Seeds grow and meadows bloom
and the woods spring anew
Sing cuckoo!

Ewe bleats after lamb,
Calf lows after cow,
Bullock leaps, billygoat farts,
Merrily sing, cuckoo!
Cuckoo, cuckoo!
Well you sing cuckoo,
Nor cease you ever now!
Sing cuckoo now, Sing, cuckoo!

– Sumer Is Icumen In (traditional English round, c. 1250).

47

I almost wish we were butterflies and liv'd but three summer days – three such days with you I could fill with more delight than fifty common years could ever contain.

– John Keats (1795–1821), one of the main figures of the second generation of Romantic poets along with Lord Byron and Percy Bysshe Shelley. This extract comes from a love letter to Fanny Brawne, posted on 3rd July 1819.

Spring flew swiftly by, and summer came; and if the village had been beautiful at first, it was now in the full glow and luxuriance of its richness. The great trees, which had looked shrunken and bare in the earlier months, had now burst into strong life and health; and stretching forth their green arms over the thirsty ground, converted open and naked spots into choice nooks, where was a deep and pleasant shade from which to look upon the wide prospect, steeped in sunshine, which lay stretched out beyond. The earth had donned her mantle of brightest green; and shed her richest perfumes abroad. It was the prime and vigour of the year; all things were glad and flourishing.

– Charles Dickens (1812–1870), *Oliver Twist; The Parish Boy's Progress* (1838). *Oliver Twist* was the first Victorian novel to feature a child protagonist, and successfully exposed the cruel treatment of many orphans who ended up destitute in large cities.

Bright was the summer's noon when quickening steps
Followed each other till a dreary moor
Was crossed, a bare ridge clomb, upon whose top
Standing alone, as from a rampart's edge,
I overlooked the bed of Windermere,
Like a vast river, stretching in the sun.
With exultation, at my feet I saw
Lake, islands, promontories, gleaming bays,
A universe of Nature's fairest forms
Proudly revealed with instantaneous burst,
Magnificent, and beautiful, and gay.

– William Wordsworth (1770–1850), 'Book Four – Summer Vacation' from *The Prelude,
or, Growth of a Poet's Mind, an Autobiographical Poem* (1850).

The animal merely makes a bed, which he warms with his body in a sheltered place; but man, having discovered fire, boxes up some air in a spacious apartment, and warms that, instead of robbing himself, makes that his bed, in which he can move about divested of more cumbrous clothing, maintain a kind of summer in the midst of winter, and by means of windows even admit the light and with a lamp lengthen out the day.

– Henry David Thoreau (1817–1862), one of the greatest of the American naturalists, 'Chapter XIII: House Warming', from *Walden; Or, Life in the Woods* (1854).

[...] Above me spreads the hot, blue mid-day sky,
Far down the hillside lies the sleeping lake
Lazily reflecting back the sun,
And scarcely ruffled by the little breeze
Which wanders idly through the nodding ferns.
The blue crest of the distant mountain, tops
The green crest of the hill on which I sit;
And it is summer, glorious, deep-toned summer,
The very crown of nature's changing year
When all her surging life is at its full.

– Amy Lowell (1874–1925), an American poet of the imagist school from Brookline,
Massachusetts. 'Summer' from *A Dome of Many-Coloured Glass* (1912).

Hark, hearer, hear what I do; lend a thought now, make believe
We are leafwhelmed somewhere with the hood
Of some branchy bunchy bushybowered wood,
Southern dene or Lancashire clough or Devon cleave,
That leans along the loins of hills, where a candycoloured, where a gluegold-brown
Marbled river, boisterously beautiful, between
Roots and rocks is danced and dandled, all in froth and waterblowballs, down.
We are there, when we hear a shout
That the hanging honeysuck, the dogeared hazels in the cover
Makes dither, makes hover
And the riot of a rout
Of, it must be, boys from the town
Bathing: it is summer's sovereign good.

– Gerard Manley Hopkins (1844–1889), an English poet, Roman Catholic convert, and
Jesuit priest. 'Epithalamion' (published in *Poems,* 1918).

Summer is only the unfulfilled promise of spring, a charlatan in place of the warm balmy nights I dream of in April. It's a sad season of life without growth... It has no day.

– F. Scott Fitzgerald (1896–1940), Eleanor speaking in 'Chapter III: Young Irony' from Book Two of *This Side of Paradise*. Published in 1920, and taking its title from a line of the Rupert Brooke poem *Tiare Tahiti*, the book examines the lives and morality of post-World War I youth.

Autumn

That time of year thou mayst in me behold
When yellow leaves, or none, or few, do hang
Upon those boughs which shake against the cold,
Bare ruined choirs, where late the sweet birds sang.
In me thou see'st the twilight of such day
As after sunset fadeth in the west;
Which by and by black night doth take away,
Death's second self, that seals up all in rest.
In me thou see'st the glowing of such fire,
That on the ashes of his youth doth lie,
As the deathbed whereon it must expire,
Consumed with that which it was nourished by.
This thou perceiv'st, which makes thy love more strong,
To love that well which thou must leave ere long.

– William Shakespeare (1564–1616), 'Sonnet 73' (1609).

Her *pleasure* in the walk must arise from the exercise and the day, from the view of the last smiles of the year upon the tawny leaves and withered hedges, and from repeating to herself some few of the thousand poetical descriptions extant of autumn–that season of peculiar and inexhaustible influence on the mind of taste and tenderness–that season which has drawn from every poet worthy of being read some attempt at description, or some lines of feeling.

– Jane Austen (1775–1817), *Persuasion* (1816); Austen's last completed novel. *Persuasion* depicts the superficial social life of Bath, a fashionable city with which Austen was well acquainted, having spent several unhappy and unproductive years there.

The thistledown's flying, though the winds are all still,
On the green grass now lying, now mounting the hill,
The spring from the fountain now boils like a pot;
Through stones past the counting it bubbles red-hot.

The ground parched and cracked is like overbaked bread,
The greensward all wracked is, bents dried up and dead.
The fallow fields glitter like water indeed,
And gossamers twitter, flung from weed unto weed.

Hill-tops like hot iron glitter bright in the sun,
And the rivers we're eying burn to gold as they run;
Burning hot is the ground, liquid gold is the air;
Whoever looks round sees Eternity there.

–John Clare (1793–1864), 'Autumn' (1821).

Go, sit upon the lofty hill,
And turn your eyes around,
Where waving woods and waters wild
Do hymn an autumn sound.
The summer sun is faint on them —
The summer flowers depart —
Sit still — as all transform'd to stone,
Except your musing heart.

How there you sat in summer-time,
May yet be in your mind;
And how you heard the green woods sing
Beneath the freshening wind.
Though the same wind now blows around,
You would its blast recall;
For every breath that stirs the trees,
Doth cause a leaf to fall.

Oh! like that wind, is all the mirth
That flesh and dust impart:
We cannot bear its visitings,
When change is on the heart.
Gay words and jests may make us smile,
When Sorrow is asleep;
But other things must make us smile,
When Sorrow bids us weep!

– Elizabeth Barrett Browning (1806–1861), one of the most prominent poets of the
Victorian era, famed for her purposeful, honest poetry. 'The Autumn' (1833).

Is not this a true autumn day? Just the still melancholy that I love – that makes life and nature harmonise. The birds are consulting about their migrations, the trees are putting on the hectic or the pallid hues of decay, and begin to strew the ground, that one's very footsteps may not disturb the repose of earth and air, while they give us a scent that is a perfect anodyne to the restless spirit. Delicious autumn! My very soul is wedded to it, and if I were a bird I would fly about the earth seeking the successive autumns.

– Mary Ann Evans (1819–1880), better known by her pen name, George Eliot. The extract comes from a letter written on 1st October, 1841, addressed to 'Miss Eliot.'

There was a filmy veil of soft dull mist obscuring, but not

hiding, all objects, giving them a lilac hue, for the sun had

not yet fully set; a robin was singing ... The leaves were more

gorgeous than ever; the first touch of frost would lay them all

low to the ground. Already one or two kept constantly floating

down, amber and golden in the low slanting sun-rays.

– Elizabeth Gaskell (1810–1865), a British novelist and short story writer. *North and South* (1854-55); dealing with the lives of the working poor separated from the natural rhythms of country-life. Gaskell described the 'misery and hateful passions caused by the love of pursuing wealth as well as the egoism, thoughtlessness and insensitivity of manufacturers.'

Know'st thou not at the fall of the leaf
How the heart feels a languid grief
   Laid on it for a covering,
   And how sleep seems a goodly thing
In Autumn at the fall of the leaf?

And how the swift beat of the brain
Falters because it is in vain,
   In Autumn at the fall of the leaf
   Knowest thou not? and how the chief
Of joys seems—not to suffer pain?

Know'st thou not at the fall of the leaf
How the soul feels like a dried sheaf
   Bound up at length for harvesting,
   And how death seems a comely thing
In Autumn at the fall of the leaf?

– Dante Gabriel Rossetti (1828–1882), founder of the *Pre-Raphaelite Brotherhood*
alongside William Holman Hunt and John Everett Millais. 'Autumn Song'
(published in 1883).

At no other time (than autumn) does the earth let itself be inhaled in one smell, the ripe earth; in a smell that is in no way inferior to the smell of the sea, bitter where it borders on taste, and more honeysweet where you feel it touching the first sounds. Containing depth within itself, darkness, something of the grave almost.

– Rainer Maria Rilke (1875–1926), *Letters on Cézanne*. Almost every day in the autumn of 1907, Rilke returned to a Paris gallery to view their exhibition on Cézanne. Just as frequently he wrote to his wife, expressing his revelations about art and life, inspired by the paintings.

Listen. . .
With faint dry sound,
Like steps of passing ghosts,
The leaves, frost-crisp'd,
break from the trees
And fall.

– Adelaide Crapsey (1878–1914), an American poet born in Brooklyn, New York.
'November Night' from *Cinquains* (1911–1913).

Winter

The wintry west extends his blast,
  And hail and rain does blaw;
Or the stormy north sends driving forth
  The blinding sleet and snaw:
While, tumbling brown, the burn comes down,
  And roars frae bank to brae;
And bird and beast in covert rest,
  And pass the heartless day.

'The sweeping blast, the sky o'ercast,'
  The joyless winter day
Let others fear, to me more dear
  Than all the pride of May:
The tempest's howl, it soothes my soul,
  My griefs it seems to join;
The leafless trees my fancy please,
  Their fate resembles mine!

Thou Power Supreme, whose mighty scheme
  These woes of mine fulfil,
Here firm I rest; they must be best,
  Because they are *Thy* will!
Then all I want—O do Thou grant
  This one request of mine!—
Since to *enjoy* Thou dost deny,
  Assist me to *resign*.

– Robert Burns (1759–1796), 'Winter: A Dirge' (1781).

O winter! bar thine adamantine doors:
The north is thine; there hast thou built thy dark
Deep-founded habitation. Shake not thy roofs
Nor bend thy pillars with thine iron car.

He hears me not, but o'er the yawning deep
Rides heavy; his storms are unchain'd, sheathed
In ribbed steel; I dare not lift mine eyes;
For he hath rear'd his sceptre o'er the world.

– William Blake (1757–1827), 'To Winter' from *Poetical Sketches* (1783). Largely
unrecognised during his lifetime, Blake is now considered a seminal figure in the history
of the poetry and visual arts of the Romantic Age.

THE WINTER WILL BE LONG AND BLEAK. NATURE HAS A DISMAL ASPECT.

– Jean Charles Emmanuel Nodier (1780–1844), a French author who introduced a younger generation of Romanticists to the *conte fantastique*, gothic literature, vampire tales, and the importance of dreams as part of literary creation.

Are the days of winter sunshine just as sad for you, too? When it is misty, in the evenings, and I am out walking by myself, it seems to me that the rain is falling through my heart and causing it to crumble into ruins.

– Gustave Flaubert (1821–1880), an influential French writer widely considered one of the greatest novelists in Western literature. *November*, a novella first published in 1842.

I wonder if the snow loves the trees and fields, that it kisses them so gently? And then it covers them up snug, you know, with a white quilt; and perhaps it says 'Go to sleep, darlings, till the summer comes again.'

– Charles Lutwidge Dodgson (1832–1898), better known as Lewis Carroll, author of *Alice's Adventures in Wonderland & Through the Looking-Glass* (1865–1871).

Late lies the wintry sun a-bed,
A frosty, fiery sleepy-head;
Blinks but an hour or two; and then,
A blood-red orange, sets again.

Before the stars have left the skies,
At morning in the dark I rise;
And shivering in my nakedness,
By the cold candle, bathe and dress.

Close by the jolly fire I sit
To warm my frozen bones a bit;
Or with a reindeer-sled, explore
The colder countries round the door.

When to go out, my nurse doth wrap
Me in my comforter and cap;
The cold wind burns my face, and blows
Its frosty pepper up my nose.

Black are my steps on silver sod;
Thick blows my frosty breath abroad;
And tree and house, and hill and lake,
Are frosted like a wedding-cake.

– Robert Louis Stevenson (1850–1894), a Scottish novelist, poet and travel writer, famed
for his novels *Treasure Island* and the *Strange Case of Dr Jekyll and Mr Hyde*. 'Winter'
from, *A Child's Garden of Verses* (1885).

It sifts from Leaden Sieves —
It powders all the Wood.
It fills with Alabaster Wool
The Wrinkles of the Road —

It makes an Even Face
Of Mountain, and of Plain —
Unbroken Forehead from the East
Unto the East again —

It reaches to the Fence —
It wraps it Rail by Rail
Till it is lost in Fleeces —
It deals Celestial Vail

To Stump, and Stack — and Stem —
A Summer's empty Room —
Acres of Joints, where Harvests were,
Recordless, but for them —

It Ruffles Wrists of Posts
As Ankles of a Queen —
Then stills its Artisans — like Ghosts —
Denying they have been —

– Emily Dickinson (1830–1886), '311 – Untitled' (c. 1864). Whilst Dickinson's output was
prolific, less than a dozen of her nearly 1800 poems were published during her lifetime.

Honest Winter, snow-clad, and with the frosted beard, I can welcome not uncordially; But that long deferment of the calendar's promise, that weeping gloom of March and April, that bitter blast outraging the honour of May how often has it robbed me of heart and hope?

– George Robert Gissing (1857–1903), an English novelist, teacher and tutor. *The Private Papers of Henry Ryecroft* (1903); a semi-fictional autobiographical work in which the author casts himself as the editor of the diary of a deceased acquaintance.

They have taken the gable from the roof of clay
On the long swede pile. They have let in the sun
To the white and gold and purple of curled fronds
Unsunned. It is a sight more tender-gorgeous
At the wood-corner where Winter moans and drips
Than when, in the Valley of the Tombs of Kings,
A boy Crawls down into a Pharaoh's tomb
And, first of Christian men, beholds the mummy,
God and monkey, chariot and throne and vase,
Blue pottery, alabaster and gold.
But dreamless long-dead Amen-hotep lies.
This is a dream of Winter, sweet as Spring

– Edward Thomas (1878–1917), 'Swedes' (date unknown). Thomas was an Anglo-
Welsh poet, particularly noted for his colloquial style and reverence for the English
countryside. Somewhat of a poetic puzzle, this particular verse describes the unassuming
root vegetable, the swede, which used to be stored in earth 'clamps.' The opening of the
swede store is compared with, and given even grander significance than the opening of a
pharaoh's tomb.

But at sunset the clouds gathered again, bringing an earlier night, and the snow began to fall straight and steadily from a sky without wind, in a soft universal diffusion more confusing than the gusts and eddies of the morning. It seemed to be a part of the thickening darkness, to be the winter night itself descending on us layer by layer.

– Edith Wharton (1862–1937), the Pulitzer Prize-winning American novelist. *Ethan Frome* (1911).

AMERICAN NATURALISTS

The greatest delight which the fields and woods minister, is the suggestion of an occult relation between man and the vegetable. I am not alone and unacknowledged. They nod to me, and I to them. The waving of the boughs in the storm, is new to me and old. It takes me by surprise, and yet is not unknown. Its effect is like that of a higher thought or a better emotion coming over me, when I deemed I was thinking justly or doing right.

Every particular in nature, a leaf, a drop, a crystal, a moment of time is related to the whole, and partakes of the perfection of the whole.

– Ralph Waldo Emerson (1803–1882), *Nature* (1836). In this essay, Emerson outlines his view of the transcendentalist movement; a belief system that espouses a 'non-traditional' appreciation of nature. Transcendentalism suggests that the divine, or God, suffuses nature, and that reality can be understood by studying nature. One can see a direct lineage from the Greek, and later Biblical scholars – to the arguments adopted by Emerson and his fellow naturalists.

Henry David Thoreau

Truth, Goodness, Beauty — those celestial thrins,

Continually are born; e'en now the Universe,

With thousand throats, and eke with greener smiles,

Its joy confesses at their recent birth.

– Thoreau's Journals, 14th June 1838. Thoreau (1817–1862) was a naturalist, poet, philosopher, abolitionist, tax resister, historian and transcendentalist. He is considered one of America's best writers on nature, for his ability to interweave close natural observation, personal experience, pointed rhetoric, symbolic meanings and historical lore.

Talk of mysteries! — Think of
our life in nature, — daily to be shown
matter, to come in contact with it, — rocks,
trees, wind on our cheeks! The *solid* earth!
the *actual* world! the *common sense! Contact!*
Contact! Who are we? *where* are we?

– *The Maine Woods*, Part XI (1848) – a collection of three essays, describing Thoreau's
trips into the Maine woods, over an eleven year period. Thoreau was deeply interested
in the idea of survival in the face of hostile elements, historical forces and natural decay.

I went to the woods because I wished to live deliberately, to front only the essential facts of life, and see if I could not learn what it had to teach, and not, when I came to die, discover that I had not lived. I did not wish to live what was not life, living is so dear; nor did I wish to practise resignation, unless it was quite necessary. I wanted to live deep and suck out all the marrow of life, to live so sturdily and Spartan- like as to put to rout all that was not life, to cut a broad swath and shave close, to drive life into a corner, and reduce it to its lowest terms, and, if it proved to be mean, why then to get the whole and genuine meanness of it, and publish its meanness to the world; or if it were sublime, to know it by experience, and be able to give a true account of it in my next excursion. For most men, it appears to me, are in a strange uncertainty about it, whether it is of the devil or of God, and have somewhat hastily concluded that it is the chief end of man here to 'glorify God and enjoy him forever'.

– *Walden* (1854). *Walden* is one of Thoreau's most famous texts, a reflection on simple living in natural surroundings. The work is part personal declaration of independence, social experiment, lived-experience of transcendentalism, satire and a manual for self-reliance. It details Thoreau's experiences over the course of two years, two months and two days in a cabin he build near Walden Pond, amidst forest owned by his friend, Ralph Waldo Emerson.

Thank you! Thank you for going a-wooding with me, – and enjoying it; – for being warmed by my wood fire. I have indeed enjoyed it much alone. I see how I might enjoy it yet more with company, – how we might help each other to live....   To be admitted to Nature's hearth costs nothing. None is excluded, but excludes himself. You only have to push aside the curtain.

– Letter to Mr. B., Concord, 9th December 1855.

Nature is full of genius, full of the divinity; so that not a snowflake escapes its fashioning hand.

– *Thoreau's Journals*, 5th January 1856. Thoreau was heavily influenced by Indian spiritual thought, and took a pantheistic approach to the world; by rejecting views of God as separate from the environment.

Life consists with wildness.
The most alive is the wildest.
Not yet subdued to man, its
presence refreshes him.

– *Walking* (1862). 'Walking' began as a lecture called 'The Wild', delivered by at the
Concord Lyceum in 1851. Thoreau gave this lecture many times, developing it into the
essay finally published in the *Atlantic Monthly* after his death, in 1862. The essay extols
the virtues of immersing oneself in nature, and laments the encroachment of private
ownership upon the wilderness (a notion which derived from Cicero's natural law).

If a man walk in the woods for love of them half of each day, he is in danger of being regarded as a loafer; but if he spends his whole day as a speculator, shearing off those woods and making earth bald before her time, he is esteemed an industrious and enterprising citizen. As if a town had no interest in its forests but to cut them down!

– *Life Without Principle* (1863). This essay was derived from the lecture 'What Shall It Profit?' which Thoreau first delivered on 6th December 1854, at Railroad Hall in Providence, Rhode Island. The lecture outlined his proposed program for a moral livelihood.

The very idea of a bird is a symbol and a suggestion to the poet. A bird seems to be at the top of the scale, so vehement and intense his life. . . . The beautiful vagabonds, endowed with every grace, masters of all climes, and knowing no bounds – how many human aspirations are realised in their free, holiday-lives – and how many suggestions to the poet in their flight and song!

– John Burroughs (1837–1921), *Birds and Poets* (1877). Burroughs abhorred the clinical detachment of 'scientific naturalism' and saw himself as a *distinctly* literary naturalist, recording his own subjective interpretations of the natural world. Nonetheless, he attacked writers such as Ernest Thompson Seton and William J. Long for what he saw as 'fantastical representations' of wildlife.

Camp out among the grass and gentians of glacier meadows, in craggy garden nooks full of Nature's darlings. Climb the mountains and get their good tidings. Nature's peace will flow into you as sunshine flows into trees. The winds will blow their own freshness into you, and the storms their energy, while cares will drop off like autumn leaves.

– John Muir (1838–1914), 'Yellowstone National Park', *Atlantic Monthly,* April 1895. A Scottish-American naturalist, and one of the most famous nature writers of all time, Muir was heavily influenced by the transcendentalism of Henry David Thoreau and Ralph Waldo Emerson, and indeed was a close friend of the latter.

The Universe is one great kindergarten for man. Everything that exists has brought with it is own peculiar lesson. The mountain teaches stability and grandeur; the ocean immensity and change. Forests, lakes, and rivers, clouds and winds, stars and flowers, stupendous glaciers and crystal snowflakes – every form of animate or inanimate existence, leaves its impress upon the soul of man. Even the bee and ant have brought their little lessons of industry and economy.

– Orison Swett Marden (1850–1924), 'Chapter XXIV', *Rising in the World: Or, Architects of Fate* (1896). Marden was an inspirational author who propounded common-sense principles and virtues that make for a 'well-rounded life.' His writings widely struck a chord with readers, encouraging them with hope and firing them with ambition to achieve.

These stories are true. Although I have left the strict line of historical truth in many places, the animals in this book were all real characters. They lived the lives I have depicted, and showed the stamp of heroism and personality more strongly by far than it has been in the power of my pen to tell.

Lobo – The King of Currumpaw...

Old Lobo, or the king, as the Mexicans called him, was the gigantic leader of a remarkable pack of gray wolves, that had ravaged the Currumpaw Valley for a number of years.... Old Lobo was a giant among wolves, and was cunning and strong in proportion to his size. His voice at night was well-known and easily distinguished from that of any of his fellows. An ordinary wolf might howl half the night about the herdsman's bivouac without attracting more than a passing notice, but when the deep roar of the old king came booming down the canon, the watcher bestirred himself and prepared to learn in the morning that fresh and serious inroads had been made among the herds.

– Ernest Thompson Seton (1860–1946), *Wild Animals I Have Known* (1898). Although British by birth, Seton moved to America in his youth, and remained there for the rest of his life. Here, he formed the Woodcraft Indians, designed to help the local adolescents of Connecticut. The story of Lobo struck a chord with the American public and played an important part in changing views towards the country's native species and the environment.

PROUD music of the storm!
Blast that careers so free, whistling across the prairies!
Strong hum of forest tree-tops! Wind of the mountains!
Personified dim shapes! you hidden orchestras!
You serenades of phantoms, with instruments alert,
Blending, with Nature's rhythmus, all the tongues of nations;
You chords left us by vast composers! you choruses!
You formless, free, religious dances! you from the Orient!
You undertone of rivers, roar of pouring cataracts;
You sounds from distant guns, with galloping cavalry!
Echoes of camps, with all the different bugle-calls!
Trooping tumultuous, filling the midnight late, bending me powerless,
Entering my lonesome slumber-chamber—Why have you seiz'd me?

– Walt Whitman (1819–1892), 'Poem no. 186. Proud Music of The Storm' from *Leaves of Grass* (1855). As a humanist, Whitman was part of the transition between the transcendentalism of Thoreau, Emerson and Muir, and the realism of later American writers such as William Dean Howells and Stephen Crane. Today, he is celebrated as one of the most influential poets in the American canon and the father of 'free verse.'

In laying before our readers this first number of a popular scientific monthly, we commence a publication in which we shall endeavour to meet the wants of all lovers of nature...

If the reader, however slight his intercourse with nature may have been, shall find something in these pages to stimulate his zeal, and direct his mind to the right methods of investigation, and also teach him new facts concerning the haunts and habits of his favourites of the wood, the lake and the seashore, the great aim of this journal will be accomplished. Should it do no more than to bring naturalists, both young and old, into an active cooperation and sympathy, and promote good fellowship and amity between the great brotherhood of enthusiasts, as all true naturalists are, we shall gain a most important object.

– 'Introduction' to the first edition of *The American Naturalist,* Vol. 1, No. 1, March 1867. Since its inception, *AmNat* has maintained its position as one of the world's premier ecological publications.

There can be no greater mistake, therefore, than to imagine an animal's life to be full of frightful alarms and haunting terrors. There is no terror in extreme watchfulness. To the animal it is simply the use of his unusual powers, with the joy and confidence that the use of unusual powers always brings, to animals as well as men. The eagle watching for prey far above his high mountain top has not more, but rather less, joy in his vision than the doe has in hers, who sees his sudden slanting flight and, knowing its meaning, hides her fawns and bids them lie still; while she runs away in plain sight, to take the robber's attention away from her little ones, and jumps for thick cover, at last, where the eagle's broad wings cannot follow. And she is not terrified, but glad as a linnet and exultant as a kingbird, when she comes cantering back again, after the danger is over.

Neither is there any terror, usually, but rather an exultant sense of power and victory in running away. Watch the deer, yonder, in his magnificent rush, light and swift as a hawk, over ground where other feet than his must halt and creep; watch the partridge in that clean, sure, curving plunge into the safety and shelter of the evergreen swamp. Hoof and wing alike seem to laugh at the danger behind, and to rejoice in their splendid power and training.

This simple fact, so glad in itself, so obvious to one who keeps his eyes open in Nature's world, is mentioned here by way of invitation – to assure the reader that, if he enter this school of the woods, he will see little truly of that which made his heart ache in his own sad world; no tragedies or footlight effects of woes and struggles, but rather a wholesome, cheerful life to make one glad and send him back to his own school with deeper wisdom and renewed courage.

– William J. Long (1866–1952), *School of the Woods* (1901). Long would leave his home in Stamford, Connecticut, every March – often with his two daughters, to travel to 'the wilderness' of Maine. They would stay until the first snows of October, though sometimes he would remain all winter. Long believed that the best way to experience the wild was to plant yourself and sit for hours on end to let the wild 'come to you; and they will!'

The Country of Lost Borders...

Ute, Paiute, Mojave, and Shoshone inhabit its frontiers, and as far into the heart of it as a man dare go. Not the law, but the land sets the limit. Desert is the name it wears upon the maps, but the Indian's is the better word. Desert is a loose term to indicate lands that support no man; whether the lands can be bitted and broken to that purpose is not proven. Void of life it never is, however dry the air and villainous the soil.

This is the nature of that country. There are hills, rounded, blunt, burned, squeezed up out of chaos, chrome and vermilion painted, aspiring to the snowline. Between the hills lie high level-looking plains full of intolerable sun glare, or narrow valleys drowned in a blue haze. The hill surface is streaked with ash drift and black, unweathered lava flows. After rains water accumulates in the hollows of small closed valleys, and, evaporating, leaves hard dry levels of pure desertness that get the local name of dry lakes. When the mountains are high and the rains heavy the pool is never quite dry, but dark and bitter, rimmed about with the efflorescence of alkaline deposits. A thin crust of it lies along the marsh over the vegetating area, which has neither beauty nor freshness.

– Mary Hunter Austin (1868–1934), *A Land of Little Rain* (1903). This book, one of Austin's finest, contains a series of interrelated lyrical essays about the flora, fauna and people of the American Southwest. Austin was able to evoke the mysticism and spirituality so particular to this region, between the High Sierra and the Mojave Desert of southern California.

... Everybody needs beauty as well as bread, places to play in and pray in, where Nature may heal and cheer and give strength to body and soul. This natural beauty-hunger is displayed in poor folks' window-gardens made up of a few geranium slips in broken cups, as well as in the costly lily gardens of the rich, the thousands of spacious city parks and botanical gardens, and in our magnificent National parks... Nevertheless, like everything else worthwhile, however sacred and precious and well-guarded, they have always been subject to attack, mostly by despoiling gain-seekers, – mischief-makers of every degree from Satan to supervisors, lumbermen, cattlemen, farmers, eagerly trying to make everything dollarable, often thinly disguised in smiling philanthropy, calling pocket-filling plunder 'Utilization of beneficent natural resources, that man and beast may be fed and the dear Nation grow great.'

– John Muir (1838–1914), 'The Tuolumne Yosemite in Danger', *The Outlook,* November 1907. Muir is widely considered as the progenitor of the environmental movement, and played a key role in establishing America's natural parks. His tireless activism helped preserve the Yosemite Valley, Sequoia National Park and many other wilderness areas.

BRITISH
NATURALISTS

Nature, that fram'd us of four elements

Warring within our breasts for regiment,

Doth teach us all to have aspiring minds.

– Christopher Marlowe (1564–1593), *Tamburlaine the Great,* Part I, Act II, scene vii (1587).

Shakespeare

When daisies pied, and violets blue,
  And lady-smocks all silver-white,
And cuckoo-buds of yellow hue
  Do paint the meadows with delight,
The cuckoo then, on every tree,
Mocks married men, for thus sings he:
    'Cuckoo!
Cuckoo, cuckoo!' O word of fear,
Unpleasing to a married ear.

– Song from _Love's Labors Lost,_ Act V, scene ii (1598).

Shall I compare thee to a summer's day?
Thou art more lovely and more temperate:
Rough winds do shake the darling buds of May,
And summer's lease hath all too short a date

Sometime too hot the eye of heaven shines,
And often is his gold complexion dimm'd;
And every fair from fair sometime declines,
By chance, or nature's changing course, untrimm'd...

– Sonnet 18 (published 1609).

If by your art, my dearest father, you have
Put the wild waters in this roar, allay them.
The sky, it seems, would pour down stinking pitch,
But that the sea, mounting to the welkin's cheek,
Dashes the fire out. O, I have suffered
With those that I saw suffer: a brave vessel,
Who had, no doubt, some noble creature in her,
Dash'd all to pieces. O, the cry did knock
Against my very heart. Poor souls, they perish'd.
Had I been any god of power, I would
Have sunk the sea within the earth or ere
It should the good ship so have swallow'd and
The fraughting souls within her.

– Miranda, *The Tempest*, Act I, scene ii (1610–11).

We that are true lovers
run into strange capers; but
as all is mortal in nature, so
is all nature in love mortal
in folly.

– Touchstone, *As You Like It*, Act II, scene iv (1599–1600).

Are not these woods
More free from peril than the envious court?

Here feel we not the penalty of Adam,
The seasons' difference, as the icy fang
And churlish chiding of the winter's wind,
Which when it bites and blows upon my body
Even till I shrink with cold, I smile, and say
'This is no flattery. These are counsellors
That feelingly persuade me what I am.'

Sweet are the uses of adversity
Which, like the toad, ugly and venomous,
Wears yet a precious jewel in his head;
And this our life, exempt from public haunt,
Finds tongues in trees, books in the running brooks,
Sermons in stones, and good in everything.

– Duke Senior, *As You Like It*, Act II, scene i (1599–1600).

Third Fisherman: ... Master, I marvel how the fishes live in the sea.

First Fisherman: Why, as men do a-land; the great ones eat up the little ones. I can compare our rich misers to nothing so fitly as to a whale; a' plays and tumbles, driving the poor fry before him, and at last devours them all at a mouthful

– Pericles, Prince of Tyre, Act II, scene i (1619).

WE CANNOT COMMAND NATURE EXCEPT BY OBEYING HER.

– Francis Bacon (1561–1626), 'Aphorism 28' from *Novum Organum* (1620). Bacon's empiricism was intended to replace the syllogisms of Aristotle – and ushered in a new relationship with the natural world. Bacon has since been compared with Dr. Faustus, the protagonist of Christopher Marlowe's play – the ever aspiring scientist who sought mastery over nature – and would stop at nothing to achieve it.

Admiring Nature in her wildest grace,
These northern scenes with weary feet I trace;
O'er many a winding dale and painful steep,
Th' abodes of coveyed grouse and timid sheep,
My savage journey, curious, I pursue,
Till fam'd Breadalbaine opens to my view.
The meeting cliffs each deep-sunk glen divides,
The woods, wild-scattered, clothe their ample sides;
Th' outstretching lake, imbosomed 'mong the hills,
The eye with wonder and amazement fills;
The Tay meandering sweet in infant pride,
The palace rising on his verdant side;
The lawns wood-fringed in Nature's native taste;
The hillocks dropt in Nature's careless haste,
The arches striding o'er the new-born stream;
The village glittering in the noontide beam.

– Robert Burns (1759–1796), 'Verses written with a Pencil over the Chimney-piece,
In the Parlour of the Inn at Kenmore, Taymouth' (1787). A pioneer of the romantic
movement, the poetry of Scotland's great bard is firmly situated in the specifics of the
Scottish nation. As Burns himself described his working method – 'I walk out, sit down
now and then, look out for objects in nature around me that are in unison or harmony
with the cogitations of my fancy and workings of my bosom, humming every now and
then the air with the verses I have framed.'

Among the singularities of this place the two rocky hollow lanes, the one to Alton, and the other to the forest, deserve our attention. These roads, running through the malm lands, are, by the traffic of ages, and the fretting of water, worn down through the first stratum of our freestone, and partly through the second; so that they look more like water-courses than roads; and are bedded with naked rag for furlongs together. In many places they are reduced sixteen or eighteen feet beneath the level of fields; and after floods, and in frosts, exhibit very grotesque and wild appearances, from the tangled roots that are twisted among the strata, and from the torrents rushing down their broken sides; and especially when those cascades are frozen into icicles, hanging in all the fanciful shapes of frost-work. These rugged gloomy scenes affright the ladies when they peep down into them from the paths above, and make timid horsemen shudder while they ride along them.

– Gilbert White (1720–1793), *The Natural History and Antiquities of Selborne* (1789).
A 'parson-naturalist', White was a pioneering English naturalist and ornithologist.
The Natural History was compiled from a mixture of letters to other naturalists, his
'Naturalist's Calendar' and systematic observations. It formed an early contribution to
British ecology and phenology, enjoyed for its charm and apparent simplicity – creating a
bucolic vision of pre-industrial England.

Nature never did betray
The heart that loved her; 'tis her privilege,
Through all the years of this our life, to lead
From joy to joy: for she can so inform
The mind that is within us, so impress
With quietness and beauty, and so feed
With lofty thoughts, that neither evil tongues,
Rash judgments, nor the sneers of selfish men,
Nor greetings where no kindness is, nor all
The dreary intercourse of daily life,
Shall e'er prevail against us, or disturb
Our cheerful faith, that all which we behold
Is full of blessings. Therefore let the moon
Shine on thee in thy solitary walk;
And let the misty mountain-winds be free
To blow against thee....

– William Wordsworth (1770–1850), 'Composed a few miles above Tintern Abbey on revisiting the banks of the Wye during a tour', 13th July 1798.

To sit in the shade on a fine day and look upon verdure is the most perfect refreshment.

– Jane Austen (1775–1817), 'Chapter IX', *Mansfield Park* (1814). Famed for her love of the quiet and secluded 'Chawton Cottage', Austen relied on the solitude of rural life to write her best novels.

The immense mountains and precipices that overhung me on every side–the sound of the river raging among the rocks, and the dashing of the waterfalls around, spoke of a power mighty as Omnipotence–and I ceased to fear, or to bend before any being less almighty than that which had created and ruled the elements, here displayed in their most terrific guise. Still, as I ascended higher, the valley assumed a more magnificent and astonishing character. Ruined castles hanging on the precipices of piny mountains; the impetuous Arve, and cottages every here and there peeping forth from among the trees, formed a scene of singular beauty. But it was augmented and rendered sublime by the mighty Alps, whose white and shining pyramids and domes towered above all, as belonging to another earth, the habitations of another race of beings...

... A tingling long-lost sense of pleasure often came across me during this journey. Some turn in the road, some new object suddenly perceived and recognised, reminded me of days gone by, and were associated with the light-hearted gaiety of boyhood. The very winds whispered in soothing accents, and maternal nature bade me weep no more.

– Mary Shelley (1797–1851), 'Chapter IX' *Frankenstein: or, The Modern Prometheus* (1818). Shelley's novel was composed following a discussion with Lord Byron on the 'nature of the principle of life.' It focuses on the student Victor Frankenstein who creates a grotesque creature – produces life – and thus works contrary to all *laws of nature.*

When once the sun sinks in the west,
And dewdrops pearl the evening's breast;
Almost as pale as moonbeams are,
Or its companionable star,
The evening primrose opes anew
Its delicate blossoms to the dew;
And, hermit-like, shunning the light,
Wastes its fair bloom upon the night,
Who, blindfold to its fond caresses,
Knows not the beauty it possesses;
Thus it blooms on while night is by;
When day looks out with open eye,
Bashed at the gaze it cannot shun,
It faints and withers and is gone.

– John Clare (1793–1864), 'Evening Primrose' (written between 1819 and 1832). Clare was known as the 'peasant poet' who celebrated simple rural life and championed its protection. He lived through an era of massive changes to both town and countryside as the Industrial Revolution swept through Europe – seeing pastures ploughed up, trees and hedges uprooted, the fens drained, and common land enclosed.

Sunday 8th December 1872

The morning had been lovely, but during our singing practice after evening Church at about half past four began the great storm of 1872. Suddenly the wind rose up and began to roar at the Tower window and shake the panes and lash the glass with torrents of rain. It grew very dark. The storm increased and we struggled home in torrents of rain and tempests of wind so fearful that we could hardly force our way across the Common to the Rectory. All the evening the roaring S.W. wind raged more and more furious... The glass cracked and strained and bent and the storm shrieked and wailed and howled like multitudes of lost spirits... The moon was high and the clouds drove wild and fast across her face. Dark storms and thick black drifts were hurrying up out of the west, where the Almighty was making the clouds his chariot and walking upon the wings of the wind. Now and then the moon looked out for a moment wild and terrified through a savage rent in the storm.

– Robert Francis Kilvert (1840–1879). Kilvert was an English clergyman remembered for his diaries reflecting rural life in the 1870s. They were published (although in edited and censored form) posthumously, to great critical acclaim.

Name and Title:	Aunt Lizzie. A lover of Nature, protector of everything in fur and feathers.
Present Position:	An aged widow, at the head of a place much too large for her bodily powers.
Educated at:	The shrine of Nature by no end of clever teachers.
Academical Distinctions:	Dame Nature does not bestow outward and visible honours, but she gives keen eyes, sharpened wits and ever-increasing pleasure.
Publications:	A great deal of rubbish of various kinds.
Recreations:	Searching for beetles and everything that flies and hops.
Address:	At home everywhere in the world of nature.

– Eliza Brightwen (1830–1906), in response to a request from 'Who's Who' magazine (date unknown). Brightwen was a Scottish naturalist, who only started writing about her wildlife research at sixty-years-old. In the late nineteenth century, Brightwen's books gained considerable popularity and she thus became a well-known figure. Demonstrating her life-long wit and humility, she replied to the questionnaire in the terms detailed above.

We often hear of bad weather, but in reality no weather is bad. It is all delightful, though in different ways. Some weather may be bad for farmers or crops, but for man all kinds are good. Sunshine is delicious, rain is refreshing, wind braces us up, snow is exhilarating...

...Rest is not idleness, and to lie sometimes on the grass under trees on a summer's day, listening to the murmur of the water, or watching the clouds float across the sky, is by no means a waste of time.

– John Lubbock (1834–1913) – banker, liberal politician, philanthropist, scientist and polymath; Chapter IV: 'Recreation', *The Use of Life* (1894).

But man is miserable and speedily lost so soon as he removes from the precincts of human art, without his shoes, without his clothes, without his dog and his gun, without an inn or a cottage to shelter him by night. Nature is worse to him than a stepmother,—he cannot love her; she is a desolate and howling wilderness. He is not a child of nature like a hare. She does not provide him a banquet and a bed upon every little knoll, every green spot of earth. She persecutes him to death if he do not return to that sphere of art to which he belongs, and out of which she will show him no mercy, but be unto him a demon of despair and a hopeless perdition.

– John Ruskin (1819–1900), quoted in the *Pacific Rural Press,* Vol. 49, No. 10, 9th March 1895. Ruskin was a pre-eminent Victorian art critic, as well as a keen naturalist, producing watercolour landscapes and penning articles on geology, ornithology and botany. Ruskin believed that the principal role of the artist was 'truth to nature.'

The study of Nature makes a man at last as remorseless as Nature.

– H.G. Wells (1866–1946), 'Chapter XIX', *The Island of Doctor Moreau* (1896).

On their lower slopes they carry the chief woods of the south country, their coombes are often fully fledged with trees, and sometimes their high places are crowned with beech or fir; but they are most admirably themselves when they are bare of all but grass and a few bushes of gorse and juniper and some yew, and their ridges make flowing but infinitely variable clear lines against the sky. Sometimes they support a plateau of flint and clay, which slopes gradually to the level of the streams. Sometimes they fall away to the vales in well-defined ledges — first a long curving slope, then a plain of cornland, and below that a steep but lesser slope covered with wood, and then again grassland or sandy heaths and rivers.

– Edward Thomas (1878–1917), *The South County* (1906); an extended reflection on the author's spiritual homeland. Thomas moved with his wife Helen to a farm at Sevenoaks Kent in 1905, before travelling on to East Hampshire and then to Gloucestershire.

ART AND
NATURE

A DIALOGUE

Scene: The library of a country house in Nottinghamshire.

Cyril: *(coming in through the open window from the terrace)*. My dear Vivian, don't coop yourself up all day in the library. It is a perfectly lovely afternoon. The air is exquisite. There is a mist upon the woods like the purple bloom upon a plum. Let us go and lie on the grass, and smoke cigarettes, and enjoy nature.

Vivian: Enjoy Nature! I am glad to say that I have entirely lost that faculty. People tell us that Art makes us love Nature more than we loved her before; that it reveals her secrets to us; and that after a careful study of Corot and Constable we see things in her that had escaped our observation. My own experience is that the more we study Art, the less we care for Nature. What Art really reveals to us is Nature's lack of design, her curious crudities, her extraordinary monotony,

her absolutely unfinished condition. Nature has good intentions, of course, but as Aristotle once said, she cannot carry them out. When I look at a landscape I cannot help seeing all its defects. It is fortunate for us, however, that Nature is so imperfect, as otherwise we should have had no art at all. Art is our spirited protest, our gallant attempt to teach Nature her proper place. As for the infinite variety of Nature, that is a pure myth. It is not to be found in Nature herself. It resides in the imagination, or fancy, or cultivated blindness of the man who looks at her...

Cyril: Well, you need not look at the landscape. You can lie on the grass and smoke and talk.

Vician: But Nature is so uncomfortable. Grass is hard and dumpy and damp, and full of dreadful black insects. Why, even Morris' poorest workman could make you a more comfortable seat than the whole of Nature can...

– Oscar Wilde, *The Decay of Lying* (1905). In this apparent invective against nature, Wilde is making the case for 'Anti-mimesis' – the philosophical position that holds the direct opposite of traditional Aristotelian mimesis (that art should imitate nature). In the essay, Wilde argues that 'Life imitates art far more than art imitates life.' He cites the example that 'one only notices the beauty and wonder of the London fog because poets and painters have taught the loveliness of such effects...They did not exist till Art had invented them.'

All the efforts of the human mind cannot exhaust the essence of a single fly.

– St. Thomas Aquinas (1225–1274)

Nature is the source of all true knowledge. She has her own logic, her own laws, she has no effect without cause nor invention without necessity.

– Leonardo da Vinci (1452–1519)

My soul can find no staircase to Heaven unless it be through Earth's loveliness.

– Michelangelo (1475–1564)

We find the Works of Nature still more pleasant, the more they resemble those of art.

– Joseph Addison (1672–1719)

The tree which moves some to tears of joy is in the eyes of others only a green thing that stands in the way. Some see nature all ridicule and deformity... and some scarce see nature at all. But to the eyes of the man of imagination, nature is imagination itself.

– William Blake (1757–1827)

There are no lines in nature, only areas of colour, one against another.

– Edouard Manet (1832–1883)

These Winter nights against my window-pane

Nature with busy pencil draws designs

Of ferns and blossoms and fine spray of pines,

Oak-leaf and acorn and fantastic vines,

Which she will make when summer comes again–

Quaint arabesques in argent, flat and cold,

Like curious Chinese etchings.

– Thomas Bailey Aldrich (1836–1907)

*The artist is the confidant of nature, flowers
carry on dialogues with him through the graceful
bending of their stems and the harmoniously tinted
nuances of their blossoms. Every flower has a
cordial word which nature directs towards him.*

– Auguste Rodin (1840–1917)

I am following Nature without being able to grasp her, I perhaps owe having become a painter to flowers.

– Claude Monet (1840–1926)

I plunged eagerly and passionately into the wilderness, as if in the hope of thus penetrating into the very heart of this Nature, powerful and maternal, there to blend with her living elements.

– Paul Gaugin (1848–1903)

When I have a terrible need of – shall I say the word – religion. Then I go out and paint the stars.

– Vincent Van Gogh (1853–1890)

Without poets, without artists, men would soon weary of nature's monotony.

– Guillaume Apollinaire (1880–1918)

FLORA
AND FAUNA

Those nimble musicians of the air, that warble forth their

curious ditties, with which nature hath furnished them to the

shame of art.

– Izaak Walton (1594–1683), *The Compleat Angler* (1653). Although an investigation into
the art and spirit of fishing, this particular paragraph celebrates the 'many and useful'
heavenly birds: the Lark, the Blackbird, the Robin and the Nightingale who 'refresh man
with their heavenly voices.'

Wee, sleekit, cow'rin, tim'rous beastie,
O, what a panic's in thy breastie!
Thou need na start awa sae hasty,
Wi' bickering brattle!
I wad be laith to rin an' chase thee,
Wi' murd'ring pattle!

I'm truly sorry man's dominion,
Has broken nature's social union,
An' justifies that ill opinion,
Which makes thee startle
At me, thy poor, earth-born companion,
An' fellow-mortal!

I doubt na, whiles, but thou may thieve;
What then? poor beastie, thou maun live!
A daimen icker in a thrave
'S a sma' request;
I'll get a blessin wi' the lave,
An' never miss't!

Thy wee bit housie, too, in ruin!
It's silly wa's the win's are strewin!
An' naething, now, to big a new ane,
O' foggage green!
An' bleak December's winds ensuin,
Baith snell an' keen!

Thou saw the fields laid bare an' waste,
An' weary winter comin fast,
An' cozie here, beneath the blast,
Thou thought to dwell –
Till crash! the cruel coulter past
Out thro' thy cell.

That wee bit heap o' leaves an' stibble,
Has cost thee mony a weary nibble!
Now thou's turn'd out, for a' thy trouble,
But house or hald,
To thole the winter's sleety dribble,
An' cranreuch cauld!

But, Mousie, thou art no thy lane,
In proving foresight may be vain;
The best-laid schemes o' mice an 'men
Gang aft agley,
An' lea'e us nought but grief an' pain,
For promis'd joy!

Still thou art blest, compar'd wi' me
The present only toucheth thee:
But, Och! I backward cast my e'e.
On prospects drear!
An' forward, tho' I canna see,
I guess an' fear!

– Robert Burns (1759–1796), 'To a Mouse' (1785). In this poem, one of Burns's finest, the author's regret at breaking 'Nature's social union' its highly reminiscent of the transcendentalism of Thoreau and Muir – that all earthly creatures are bound together through compassionate exchange.

O Rose thou art sick.
The invisible worm,
That flies in the night
In the howling storm:

Has found out thy bed
Of crimson joy:
And his dark secret love
Does thy life destroy.

– William Blake (1757–1827), 'The Sick Rose' from *Songs of Innocence and Experience* (1789–1794). Blake often represented 'fallen man' and the hypocritical nature of the human condition – here reflected in the innocence of the corrupted rose.

Ten thousand warblers cheer the day, and one
The live-long night. Not those alone whose notes
Nice-finger'd art must emulate in vain;
But crawing rooks, and kites, that swim sublime
In still repeated circles, screaming loud;
The jay, the pie, and e'en the boding owl,
That hails the rising moon, have charms for me.

– William Cowper (1731–1800), 'Untitled' quoted in *The Works of William Cowper* (1835).
One of the most popular poets of his time, Cowper significantly changed the direction of
eighteenth century nature poetry by writing on everyday life and scenes of the English
countryside. He was a forerunner of the Romantic works of Coleridge and Wordsworth
– the latter of whom particularly admired Cowper's poem *Yardley-Oak*.

The wood, the mountain, and the barren waste, the craggy rock, the river and the lake, are never searched in vain; each have their peculiar inhabitants, that enliven the scene and please the philosophic eye.

– George Montagu (1753–1815), *Ornithological Dictionary* (1802). This text was the first attempt to accurately define the status of Britain's birds, resulting in the species 'Montagu's Harrier' being named after him.

'Tis the last rose of summer

Left blooming alone;

All her lovely companions

Are faded and gone;

No flower of her kindred,

No rosebud is nigh,

To reflect back her blushes,

To give sigh for sigh...

– Thomas Moore (1779–1852), 'The Last Rose of Summer' (1805). Roses, and their links to love and life, have been a constant source of fascination to nature writers. Moore was an Irish poet, singer and songwriter and this touching poem is one of his best known works – evoking the melancholy and loneliness felt as old age grows near.

We often wandered in the recesses of our woods and the passes of far-stretching and craggy mountains, searched around our wild or beautiful lakes and our precipitous sea-coasts, and we have never been disappointed. If we did not always meet with some species new to our collection, we found fresh facts to record of those we already possessed; and we delighted in the landscape enlivened by the airy creatures whose structure we had been examining, and whose habits we could there survey so freely. What would the landscape be without its living inhabitants? The luxuriance of vegetation, varying with beautiful flowers and rich foliage, has charms quiet and seducing, and affording ample subject for contemplation. In the depth of the forest, or on the mountain top, ere break of day had awakened their various tenants and in some of our beautiful mornings of mid-year, we have seen how deeply tinted seemed the green of the foliage, and how chaste and blended were the tints on the nearly barren rock; how lovely the sylvan flowers appeared, showing their freshest blossoms amidst the soft and matted growth beneath, and how exquisite the structure of the moss or lichen within our reach; how calm, clear and serene the air, how deep the shadows, but how complete the quiet, how still the silence!

– Sir William Jardine (1800–1874), 'Ornithology, Vol. I, Birds of Great Britain and Ireland.' *The Naturalist's Library* (1838). A Scottish Baronet, Jardine made natural history available to all levels of Victorian society by editing and issuing the hugely popular forty volumes of *The Naturalist's Library* (1833–1848). Jardine was also responsible for an edition of Gilbert White's *Natural History of Selborne,* which re-established White's reputation.

The badger grunting on his woodland track
With shaggy hide and sharp nose scrowed with black
Roots in the bushes and the woods, and makes
A great high burrow in the ferns and brakes.
With nose on ground he runs an awkward pace,
And anything will beat him in the race.

The shepherd's dog will run him to his den
Followed and hooted by the dogs and men.
The woodman when the hunting comes about
Goes round at night to stop the foxes out
And hurrying through the bushes to the chin
Breaks the old holes, and tumbles headlong in....

– John Clare (1793–1864), 'The Badger' (date unknown). A commentary on (though not
necessarily condemnation of) the cruelty of man against nature.

Ferns are found in almost and every part of the globe where vascular vegetation exists at all; but they are chiefly abound in moist and warm climates. They have a peculiar habit, by which they are more easily to be recognised than described, differing greatly from all other vegetables, generally exhibiting the most graceful forms, and varying in size from the humble *Trichomanes* or *Hymenophyllum* to the noble Tree-Ferns of the equatorial Forests.

Subord. I. – Gleicheniaceae, Br.

Suri dorsal, naked, subglobose, formed of a few, sessile, sometimes immersed capsules, which have a transverse or obliquely transverse, complete, clastic ring, bursting vertically (from the apex.) – Tropical; or extra-tropical *only in the southern hemisphere, of a harsh and rigid texture, simple or, generally, with copious, dichotomous branches, and gemmae in the axils, the ultimate branches pinnatifid.*

– William Hooker (1785–1865), *Species Filicum* – 'Species of Ferns' (5 vols., 1846–1864). 'Nature writing' as it has generally been espoused in this book, owes a great debt to early botanists such as Hooker. Not only a systematic observer (and painstaking reporter!) of the natural world, Hooker was also a gifted illustrator and his drawings vastly improved our understanding of British and exotic flora, but most especially – ferns.

Loveliest of trees, the cherry now

Is hung with bloom along the bough.

And stands about the woodland ride

Wearing white for Eastertide.

Now, of my threescore years and ten,

Twenty will not come again,

And take from seventy springs a score,

It only leaves me fifty more.

And since to look at things in bloom

Fifty springs are little room,

About the woodlands I will go

To see the cherry hung with snow.

– A. E. Housman (1859–1936), 'Loveliest of Trees, the Cherry now' from, *A Shropshire Lad* (1896). A cycle of sixty–three poems, Housman's lyrical and almost epigrammatic verses wistfully evoke the nostalgia of youth in the English countryside. Their beauty and simplicity appealed strongly to late Victorian and Edwardian taste, and have ever since been closely associated with that era and Shropshire itself.

Everything is blooming most recklessly; if it were voices instead of colours, there would be an unbelievable shrieking into the heart of the night.

– Rainer Maria Rilke (1875–1926), *Letters of Rainer Maria Rilke*, 1892–1926. A Bohemian-Austrian poet and novelist, Rilke's work is intense and mystical, often depicting the difficulty of communing with the natural world in the modern, cynical age.

As one who has hunted the Lily on cliff and dale, on mountain-slope and alpine moorland, and through woodland and swamp in many remote parts of China and the Tibetan borderland, and from the extreme south of Japan northward through that pretty country to Saghalien and the lonely shores of the Okhotsk Sea, I propose here to consider, cursorily, how Lilies grow. No class of herbs is more widely known or more highly appreciated; on no class of plants is more money annually spent (I had almost written wasted); and with no class of flowers do amateurs succeed less. The Lily growers who have achieved outstanding success can be counted on one's fingers, and nurserymen have failed as completely as have amateurs.

– Ernest Henry Wilson (1876–1930), *Aristocrats of the Garden* (1917) – from a chapter titled 'Consider the Lilies', in reference to the biblical allusion in Luke 12:27. Just as the bible passage preaches the vainness of working for worldly, luxurious pleasures – Seton discusses the at times ineffable nature of horticultural growing.

FORESTS AND FOOTHILLS

For in the true nature of things, if we rightly consider, every green tree is far more glorious than if it were made of gold and silver.

– Martin Luther (1483–1546); a German monk and Catholic priest – and founding father of the Protestant reformation.

At summer eve, when Heav'n's aerial bow
Spans with bright arch the glittering hills below,
Why to yon mountain turns the musing eye,
Whose sun-bright summit mingles with the sky?
Why do those cliffs of shadowy tint appear
More sweet than all the landscape smiling near? –
'Tis distance lends enchantment to the view,
And robes the mountain in its azure hue.

– Thomas Campbell (1777–1844), 'The Pleasures of Hope' (1799). Campbell was a
Scottish poet chiefly remembered for his sentimental, romantic poetry. This work, a
didactic poem composed in heroic couplets dealt with subjects as diverse as the French
revolution, the partition of Poland, and slavery.

There is a pleasure in the pathless woods,
There is a rapture on the lonely shore,
There is society, where none intrudes,
By the deep sea, and music in its roar:
I love not man the less, but Nature more,
From these our interviews, in which I steal
From all I may be, or have been before,
To mingle with the Universe, and feel
What I can ne'er express, yet cannot all conceal.

– Lord Byron (1788–1824), *Childe Harold's Pilgrimage* – a lengthy narrative poem written
in four parts and published between 1812 and 1818. Regarded as one of the greatest
British poets of all time, Lord Byron was a leading figure in the Romantic movement, and
championed its drive against the scientific rationalisation of nature.

'Where Alps o'er Alps arise,' tossing about their billowy

tops, and tumbling their unwieldy shapes in all directions – a

world of wonders! – Any one, who is much of an egotist, ought

not to travel through these districts; his vanity will not find its

account in them; it will be chilled, mortified, shrunk up: but

they are a noble treat to those who feel themselves raised in

their own thoughts and in the scale of being by the immensity

of other things, and who can aggrandise and piece out their

personal insignificance by the grandeur and eternal forms

of nature!

– William Hazlitt (1778–1830), 'First view of the Alps' from *Notes of a Journey through France and Italy* (1826). Hazlitt is largely remembered for his humanistic essays, social commentary and literary criticism – the 'greatest critic of his age.'

MOUNTAINS ARE THE BEGINNING AND THE END OF ALL NATURAL SCENERY.

– John Ruskin (1819–1900), *Modern Painters,* vol. IV, part 5 (1856).

I do not think we ever estimate the woods highly enough, ever know their real worth, until we find some favourite retreat levelled to the ground, and then feel the void and irreparable blankness which is left. Consider too, the purposes to which Nature turns her woods, either softening the horrors of precipice, or adorning spaces which else would be utterly without interest, or adding beauty to beauty. Consider, further, how she beguiles us when we are in them, leading us forward, each little rise appearing a hill, because we cannot see its full extent; how too, the paths close behind us, shutting us out with their silent doorways from all noise and turmoil, whilst the soft green light fills every dim recess, and deepens each pillared aisle, the floor paved with the golden mosaic of the sunlight.

– John Richard de Capel Wise (1831–1890), *The New Forest: Its History and Its Scenery* (1863).

Its not so much for its beauty that the forest makes a claim upon men's hearts, as for that subtle something, that quality of air that emanation from old trees, that so wonderfully changes and renews a weary spirit.

– Robert Louis Stevenson (1850–1894), in *Forest Notes* (1875–1876). Famed for such works as *Treasure Island* and the *Strange Case of Dr Jekyll and Mr Hyde,* Stevenson was also an avid travel writer, especially fond of the Forest of Fontainebleau – about sixty kilometres southeast of Paris.

It is winter in the pine-wood, and the giant limbs of the trees stand starkly outlined against the sky. Nought but silence possesses the aisle of plumed pines. They are hoary with their white weight of snow. The woods are painful in their very stillness, and except for the faint trickle of the stream it would seem almost as though the pulse of Nature had ceased to beat.

– 'Pine-Wood Studies: The Coming of the Crossbills' in, *Woodlanders and Field Folk – Sketches of Wild Life in Britain* (1907) by John Watson and Blanche Winder.

When the beauty of the Aster displaces that of the Goldenrod in September; when blue and purple transcend the yellow in field and border; the deep green mantle of foliage draping hill and dale, mountain and ravine, streamside and roadside, commences to show signs of portentous change. The Pines, the Hemlocks and their kin look even darker and the contrast with their deciduous-leaved neighbours becomes stronger. In the swamps about the last week of August and at the first whiff of autumn in the air the Red Maple begins to assume a purplish tint and its example is soon followed by other kinds of trees. To all of us the season of the year becomes apparent, warning signs of stern winter's approach increase rapidly and soon the whole country puts on its gayest mantle of colour.... No scene in nature is more delightful than the woods of eastern North America in the fullness of their Autumn splendour.

– Ernest Henry Wilson (1876–1930), 'The Glory of Autumn – The wonderful colouring of the passing leaves, and what it means', from *Aristocrats of the Garden* (1917).

Every walk to the woods is a religious rite, every bath in the stream is a saving ordinance. Communion service is at all hours, and the bread and wine are from the heart and marrow of Mother Earth.

– John Burroughs (1837–1921), *The Faith of a Naturalist* (1919). This quotation perfectly demonstrates Burroughs' pantheistic, highly individual approach to the natural world.

God has cared for these trees, saved them from

drought, disease, avalanches, and a thousand tempests

and floods. But he cannot save them from fools.

– John Muir (1838–1914), 'Chapter 10' from *Our National Parks* (1901).

What would be ugly in a garden constitutes beauty in a mountain.

– Victor Marie Hugo (1802–1885), 'Thoughts: Postscriptum de ma Vie' from *Victor Hugo's Intellectual Autobiography* (1907). One of the best known French writers of all time, Victor Hugo was also a keen painter, often depicting surreal, slightly abstract landscapes.

Trees are the earth's endless effort to speak to the listening heaven.

– Rabindranath Tagore (1861–1941), *Fireflies* (1928).

SKIES
AND SEAS

I know the stars by heart,

the armies of the night, and there in the lead the

ones that bring us snow or the crops of summer,

bring us all we have—

our great blazing kings of the sky, I know them,

when they rise and when the fall…

– Aeschylus (c. 525/524 BC – c. 456/455 BCE). 'Agamemnon', the first part of *The Oresteia* (458 BCE) – the only complete (save a few missing lines in several parts) trilogy of Greek plays still extant.

According to the account of Fabianus, the deepest sea has a depth of nearly two miles... This is rendered more remarkable by springs of fresh water bubbling out as if from pipes on the seashore. In fact the nature of water also is not deficient in marvels. Patches of fresh water float on the surface of the sea, being doubtless lighter. Consequently also seawater being of a heavier nature gives more support to objects floating upon it. But some fresh waters too float on the surface of others... Some rivers so hate the sea that they actually flow underneath the bottom of it, for instance the spring Arethusa at Syracuse, in which things emerge that have been thrown into the Alpheus which flows through Olympia and reaches the coast in the Peloponnese.

– Pliny the Elder (23–79 CE), *Naturalis Historia*, Book II, CVI.

Mortal as I am, I know that I am born for a day.
But when I follow at my pleasure the serried multitude
of the stars in their circular course, my feet no longer
touch the earth.

> – Claudius Ptolemy (90–168 CE), the Greco-Egyptian writer of Alexandria, known
> as a mathematician, astronomer, geographer, and poet of a single epigram in the
> Greek Anthology.

He that will enjoy the brightness of sunshine, must quit the coolness of the shade.

– Samuel Johnson (1709–1784), 'Taxation No Tyranny' (1775). Previously an opponent of the British government, this quotation comes from an essay (part of a series of pamphlets) in favour of various government policies. *Taxation* was a response to the American Declaration of Rights which protested against taxation without representation.

If I had to choose a religion, the sun as the universal giver of life would be my god.

– Napoleon Bonaparte (1769–1821) – Emperor of the French from 1804 to 1815.

The misery of man appears like childish petulance, when we explore the steady and prodigal provision that has been made for his support and delight on this green ball which floats him through the heavens. What angels invented these splendid ornaments, these rich conveniences, this ocean of air above, this ocean of water beneath, this firmament of earth between? This zodiac of lights, this tent of dropping clouds, this striped coat of climates, this fourfold year?

– Ralph Waldo Emerson (1803–1882), 'Chapter II' from *Nature* (1836).

... My soul is full of longing

For the secret of the sea,

And the heart of the great ocean

Sends a thrilling pulse through me.

– Henry Wadsworth Longfellow (1807–1882) – an American lyrical poet, famed for his musicality and mythology. This extract is taken from 'The Secret of the Sea', part of *The Seaside and The Fireside* collection (1850).

The most vivacious, and therefore the most amusing of the denizens of this floating forest that I found, were the different sorts of crabs and shrimps that abounded in it. Their numbers, their variety, the brilliant hues of many, the peculiarities of structure that fitted them for an ocean-life, the instincts which impelled the strong to prey on the weaker, and the latter to escape, with the watchfulness, cunning, agility, and artful devices continually brought into exercise by both parties in this predatory warfare, afforded an instructive entertainment for many an hour.

– Philip Henry Gosse (1810–1888), *Letters from Alabama, chiefly relating to Natural History* (1859). As well as a popular naturalist, Gosse was also the inventor of the seawater aquarium, and a painstaking innovator in the study of marine biology.

It is written on the arched sky; it looks out from every star; it is on the sailing cloud and in the invisible wind; it is among the hills and valleys of the earth, where the shrubless mountain-top pierces the thin atmosphere of eternal winter, or where the mighty forest fluctuates before the strong wind with its dark waves of green foliage; it is spread out, like a legible language, upon the broad face of the unsleeping ocean; it is the poetry of nature; it is this which uplifts the spirit within us until it is strong enough to overlook the shadows of our place of probation.

– John Ruskin (1819–1900), 'The poetry of nature' from *Modern Painters* (1843–60). The text was primarily written as a defence of the later work of J.M.W Turner, and contends that art should devote itself to the accurate documentation of nature. In Ruskin's view Turner had developed from early detailed representations of nature to a more profound insight into natural forces and atmospheric effects.

The sea is everything. It covers seven tenths of the globe. Its breath is pure and healthy. It is an immense desert, where man is never lonely, for he feels life stirring on all sides. The sea is only the embodiment of a supernatural and wonderful existence. It is nothing but love and emotion; it is the Living Infinite.

– Jules Verne (1828–1905), *Twenty Thousand Leagues Under the Sea* (1870) – the story of Captain Nemo and his submarine *Nautilus* on an adventure around the world's oceans.

I believe a leaf of grass is no less than the journey-work of the stars.

– Walt Whitman (1819–1892), *Leaves of Grass* (1855).

Ocean: A body of water occupying about two-thirds of a world made for man – who has no gills.

– Ambrose Bierce (1842–1914), *The Devil's Dictionary* (1911). Bierce was an American editorialist, journalist and short story writer, most famed for his satirical lexicon, *The Devil's Dictionary*. His motto 'nothing matters' alongside his sardonic view of human nature and the wider world earned him the nickname 'Bitter Bierce.'

There's nothing like the sun as the year dies
Kind as it can be, this world being made so,
To stones and men and beasts and birds and flies,
To all things that it touches except snow,
Whether on mountain side or street of town...

– Edward Thomas (1878–1917), 'There's nothing like the Sun' (1915). Thomas was killed
in action during the Battle of Arras in 1917, soon after he arrived in France. Two years
earlier, he was posted to Hare Hall Camp in Essex, where he served as a map-reading
instructor for officers. It was during his time at Hare Hall that he wrote this poem.

When I gaze at a sunset sky and spend hours contemplating its marvellous
ever-changing beauty, an extraordinary emotion overwhelms me. Nature in
all its vastness is truthfully reflected in my sincere though feeble soul... To feel
the supreme and moving beauty of the spectacle to which Nature invites her
ephemeral guests! ... that is what I call prayer.

– Claude Debussy (1862–1918), as quoted in *Claude Debussy: His Life and Works* (1933)
by Léon Vallas. Alongside Maurice Ravel, Debussy was one of the most prominent
figures associated with Impressionist music (though he himself disliked the term) – this
was composition with a focus on suggestion and atmosphere; conveying moods and
emotions rather than 'detailed tone pictures.'

I know not where the white road runs, nor what the blue hills are,

But man can have the sun for friend, and for his guide a star;

And there's no end of voyaging when once the voice is heard,

For the river calls and the road calls, and oh, the call of a bird!

– Gerald Gould (1885–1936), 'Wander Thirst' (date unknown). Gould was an English journalist, essayist and poet.

Poetry makes nothing happen.

– W.H. Auden

The Writers On... Series hopes to show that words, crafted well, with thought, precision and imagination, can have a lasting impact on the world around us.

A good quotation can illuminate meaning, provide evidence or inspiration, pay homage or merely make the user seem well-read.

But what is the importance of being 'well-read'? Literature, although pleasing and entertaining in itself, is so much more than that. Like all the creative arts, it preserves ideals, and is often the last thing left to speak across the ages. It makes the otherwise non-existent, un-envisaged, and un-spoken widely available. As W.H. Auden so aptly states, 'Poetry makes nothing happen.' And this nothingness is exactly the point. With the act of reading, good writing makes the previously un-imagined, *possible*. Through poetry and prose, nothing becomes something.

Dealing with any aspect of our daily lives, from serious topics such as love and the environment, to sensual pleasures such as food, drink or sex – it is good to bear in mind those words which have peaked our awareness. With this collection of some of the greatest, *Writers On...* the reader will hopefully never be short of possibilities.

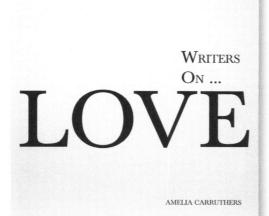

WRITERS
ON ...

LOVE

AMELIA CARRUTHERS

WRITERS
ON ...

ATHEISM

AMELIA CARRUTHERS

WRITERS
ON ...

FOOD

AMELIA CARRUTHERS

WRITERS
ON ...

SEX

AMELIA CARRUTHERS

Printed in Great Britain
by Amazon